ELIZABETH EINBERG

GAINSBOROUGH'S *Giovanna Baccelli*

THE TATE GALLERY

Exclusively distributed in France and Italy by Idea Books
46–8 rue de Montreuill, 75011 Paris and Via Cappuccio 21, 20123 Milan

ISBN 0 905005 60 0
Published by order of the Trustees 1976
for the exhibition of 3 November–12 December 1976
Copyright © 1976 The Tate Gallery
Published by the Tate Gallery Publications Department,
Millbank, London SWIP 4RG
Designed by Pauline Key
Blocks by Augustan Engravers, London
Printed in Great Britain by Balding & Mansell Ltd, Wisbech, Cambs.

Contents

Cover
Thomas Gainsborough, *Giovanna Baccelli*
Catalogue No.10

The acquisition last year of Gainsborough's magnificent full-length portrait of Giovanna Baccelli has provided us with this opportunity of organising an exhibition devoted to the sitter, a lady of great reputation in the late eighteenth century both as a dancer and as mistress of the 3rd Duke of Dorset.

The exhibition has been selected and the catalogue written by Elizabeth Einberg of the Tate Gallery who has put together some fascinating new material on Madame Baccelli.

We are most grateful to Lord Sackville for his generous support of this project without which the exhibition could not have taken place.

We also owe special thanks for the untiring help and enthusiastic support given by the following: Dr Felix Hull and Miss Elizabeth Melling of the Kent Record Office; Dr Peter Walne and Miss A. Pegrum of the Hertfordshire Record Office; Mr and Mrs Hugh Sackville West; Mr M. J. Downing and Miss K. Bryon of Barclays Bank Ltd; Miss Anne Turner; Mr Edward Croft-Murray; Miss Bridget Egerton; Mr Nigel Arch of the National Army Museum, and Mr Raymond Mander of the Mander and Mitchenson Theatre Collection.

Norman Reid *Director*

Lenders

Giovanna Baccelli

Giovanna Francesca Antonia Guiseppe Zanerini, commonly called Baccelli, to give her her full legal name, must have been a woman of extraordinary charm. From her numerous portraits one can see that she was not outstandingly beautiful, yet her liaisons were of unusually long duration, she appears to have been on good terms with the wives of her more respectable gentlemen friends, and her servants stayed with her for life. Contemporary gossips, who generally liked to hone the cutting edge of their wit on the queens of the demi-monde, are remarkably gentle with La Baccelli. The recurring adjectives are 'elegant', 'graceful', 'admirable', 'sweet-tempered' and even, at the end of her life, 'benevolent'. She was also a very good ballet dancer.

Of her origins we know little, save that she was born in Venice and that her stage name Baccelli was also that of her mother. We do not know if she was related to the singer Domenico Baccelli who surfaces briefly in the annals of the Paris Opéra in the 1760s and 70s, but from the fluency of her French one suspects that she received her training in France. One would, indeed, expect this to be so, as French dancers dominated the stages throughout Europe and it was through French ballet-masters, notably Noverre and Gaëtan and Auguste Vestris, that ballet was to develop, towards the end of the eighteenth century, from a decorative adjunct of the opera into an independent art form.

The first firm date connected with her is the 19 November 1774, when she appeared as the Rose in *Le Ballet des Fleurs* at the

King's Theatre, Haymarket. She remained with the company—except when she danced abroad, which was often–until 1789, when she returned from Italy to find that the theatre had burnt down. The company recovered within a year, but, as far as we know, by that time Baccelli had given up dancing for good.

In the years between, she performed regularly at the King's Theatre, the Paris Opéra, and in Venice, Florence and other places, which involved long and arduous journeying that, bearing in mind the travelling conditions of the time, must have required the endurance of a camel.

Nor was her social life very restful. Most successful ballerinas of her day belonged to what the newspapers called 'the higher order of impures' and the accounts of their doings have a flavour of Hollywood in its heyday: 'The Bird of Paradise [probably Baccelli's colleague Mlle Theodore] is figuring away in very elegant luxury' writes the *Morning Herald* on 20 April 1782, 'upon the income of 1,200 l. per ann. allowed her by her generous friend. Her drawing-room is at this season stocked with roses and pinks in full bloom, and in quantity sufficient to supply a moderate garden in the month of June'. The silly season is filled with descriptions of their hats, their splendid carriages, their summer retreats. Exactly when Baccelli reached the higher echelons of this band we do not know, but by 1779 she had arrived, for in October that year her address was one of the best in England: Knole, Sevenoaks, the seat of John Frederick Sackville, 3rd Duke of Dorset.

The Duke inherited title, fortune and estates from his uncle at the age of twenty-four in 1769, and, while fully sharing his uncle's lavish interest in the stage and opera, soon reversed the process of creeping disrepair into which the estate had fallen. He bought for it sculpture and paintings while on his grand tour, stocked it with vast quantities of plate and silver and extended his patronage to a host of living artists like Reynolds, Opie,

There were . . . several striking likenesses among the portraits, [such] as Gainsborough's Madame Baccelli.

Review of Royal Academy exhibition, *Westminster Magazine*, May 1782. (Whitley papers, British Museum)

This favourite Performer has been the Object of so much deserved Admiration, she is usually seen with so many Advantages from Dress &c. that it would be difficult for any Painter to do her Justice in the opinion of her Friends. Mr. Gainsborough, by not aiming at more than Justice, has hardly given a Likeness. The Figure, however, is as the Original, light airy and elegant.

Review of Royal Academy exhibition, *St James's Chronicle*, 30 April–2 May 1782 (Whitley papers, British Museum)

Gainsborough's Baccelli is, as we told our Readers before it was seen in public a good moral *likeness.–The same Artist's Head of* Dally [Mrs Elliott, later known as Mme St. Alban] *is to be mentioned in the opposite way; it is not a good moral Likeness; – the* Eyes *are too characteristic of her Vocation.*

Review of Royal Academy exhibition, *The Public Advertiser*, 2 May 1782 (Whitley papers, British Museum)

Review of Royal Academy exhibition, *Gazetteer*, 1 May 1782

Review of ballet 'Apelles and Campaspe', *Morning Herald*, 7 June 1782

Humphry, Romney, Hoppner and, of course, Gainsborough. But by and large his life revolved round the balls and masquerades, levées and receptions of aristocratic society in London, Paris and Rome, and his letters are couched in that curious *franglais* that seems to have been the *lingua franca* of the eighteenth-century equivalent of what today would be described as the international jet-set. Endowed with remarkably good looks and a manner that was 'soft, quiet and ingratiating', set off by habits of princely extravagance and aristocratic self-assurance, he proved irresistible to women and had a succession of famous mistresses, of whom Nancy Parsons, Mrs Elizabeth Armistead, Lady Betty Hamilton (later Countess of Derby) and, last and longest, Giovanna Baccelli, were the most notable.

In 1783 he was appointed British ambassador in Paris, a post that he retained until the French Revolution, but his background had hardly fitted him for serious political tasks. These were kept to a minimum, while he continued his lavish entertainments and patronage of the Paris Opéra, with Baccelli at his side. His dispatches are filled with things like the affair of the Queen's necklace, Montgolfier's dirigible balloon, and string-pulling for the Order of the Garter, which honour, he felt, was overdue to him. When he finally received it in 1788, Walpole gleefully noted that he let the Baccelli dance at the Opéra wearing the Garter ribbon as a bandeau round her head. He was favoured with the friendship of Marie Antoinette for whom he fulfilled many trivial commissions like supplying her with English gloves, and some of the 'cups of the late Queen of France' that Baccelli held among her most treasured possessions at her death must have been a sad memento of this time.

Nothing in this existence warned him that the order of things could change. His health undermined by high living and the after-effects of a slight stroke in 1785, the clouds of hereditary melancholia must have already appeared on the horizon. The affectionate tone in which he writes of Giovanna Baccelli at this time shows that her natural sweetness of temper and vivacity must have been a great antidote for gathering depression. The events of the Revolution shattered him completely, he asked to be relieved of his duties and from then on his mind sought stability in the administration of his estates, in the continuation of the Sackville line through a respectable marriage to the heiress Arabella Diana Cope, and in the conservation of his wealth through stringent economy. Giovanna Baccelli no longer fitted into this life and in December 1789 she departed from Knole for good, leaving behind her her son by the Duke and a faint echo of her name – 'Shelley's Tower' – attached henceforward to her former suite of rooms. The parting seems to have been amicable and was probably much eased by her long-standing friendship with Henry Herbert, 10th Earl of Pembroke, whose scandalous life abroad and at home reads like a more robust version of the Duke of Dorset's. After the Earl's death in 1794, Baccelli settled, appropriately, in Sackville Street, off Piccadilly, with a Mr James Carey, who took good care of her affairs and was still alive in 1827. Meanwhile the Duke was gradually declining into a depressive state that was only relieved, so tradition has it, by music being played softly in a neighbouring room, until, in 1799, he died in a state of 'mental alienation' at the age of 54.

Giovanna Baccelli lived two years longer, surrounded by prints and paintings of herself, the Duke and the Earl of Pembroke, French *objets d'art* and her faithful servants, and cheered by the inhabitants of a no doubt exquisite bird-cage. If her past was frivolous, this does not show in the thoughtful and practical dispositions of her will, in which her small fortune was distributed among those servants and relatives who could be expected to depend on her in a way that can only be described as 'benevolent'.

Baccelli meets the highest admiration in Paris, the splendor of her equipage and dress is recommended by a nobless-kind of parade. She gives suppers twice a week in the first style, and directs her attention, while she presides at the fête, chiefly to her English visitors.

Morning Herald (quoted by Ivor Guest, *Ballet Annual*, 1957)

Madame Baccelli lives in great splendour in Paris, and no lady more truly deserves good fortune than herself. Her house is the resort of all the fashionable English in that gay metropolis; and it is the chief pleasure and study of her life, to shew her gratitude to our nation for the protection with which she was honoured by our nobility.

Morning Herald, 9 February 1785

Madame St. Alban is at this time sitting to Mr. Gainsborough and surveys, with triumphant air, the portrait of the toe-poised Baccelli, which is placed in the Gallery of that distinguished painter.

Morning Herald, 29 June 1785 (Whitley papers, British Museum)

Gainsborough's 'Giovanna Baccelli'

In his younger days the 3rd Duke of Dorset positively enjoyed the company of artists, be they painters, musicians, dancers or singers, and even in his morose declining years he played at Casino with a rather nervous Hoppner when the latter stayed at Knole to paint the Duke's three children. Hoppner won fifteen shillings off him, and was disturbed by the way the Duke fretted about this. The days of the Duke's lavish patronage had passed, but by this time Knole had already accumulated, thanks to him, those treasures of the eighteenth-century British school for which it is still famous.

Highest in the Duke's esteem was the courtly Sir Joshua Reynolds, by whom he had himself painted in his peer's robes upon inheriting the title in 1769. For the rest of his life, he continued to add to his collection of Reynolds paintings until there were enough of them to fill a 'Reynolds Room'. In 1780 Reynolds presented the Duke with a replica of his Uffizi self-portrait, and when Reynolds died in 1792, the Duke was one of the pall-bearers at his funeral.

No such mutual esteem existed, as far as we know, between the Duke and Gainsborough. The five paintings ordered from him for Knole (of which only the magnificent portrait of the Duke remains *in situ*) are covered in one receipt of 1784 by the sum of £105, which is so low that one hopes it may be only a part-payment, though this is not stated (the Duke had paid £400 for Reynolds' 'Ugolino' in 1773).

It is possible that the initiative of being portrayed by Gainsborough came from Baccelli herself, rather than the Duke, for we find that Gainsborough had already a more than casual connection with Baccelli's theatre, the King's in Haymarket, usually known as the Opera House. Gainsborough, as is well known, was a keen amateur musician, and friendly, from his Bath days, with

Sheridan. In 1778 Sheridan became part owner of the King's Theatre, and thus on 25 November that year the *Morning Chronicle* could write, describing the new management's improvements, that 'The sides of the frontispiece are decorated with two figures painted by Gainsborough which are remarkably picturesque and beautiful . . .'. The *Morning Post* of 30 November adds that the figures are painted in white, on the side wings before the curtain, and represent 'Music' and 'Dancing'. This represents some precedent in the subject matter of the dance, rare in British art generally, and in Gainsborough's usually straightforward portraiture particularly so. One does not normally associate allegorical or decorative paintings with Gainsborough, yet they are not unknown: 'A Comic Muse by Gainsborough is most highly spoken of' writes Mrs Harris in February 1775, describing Bach's new concert hall in London (quoted in Whitley, p.114). In 1784 the *Morning Herald* bemoaned the disappearance of the two figures in a new bout of redecoration at King's, but already on 9 November 1782 the *Morning Chronicle* wanted to know where Gainsborough's 'fine figure of Comic Dancing' had disappeared to, and suggested that it had been removed from the Opera House because every dancer on the stage suffered by comparison.

Towards the end of his life, in the 1780s, Gainsborough's style was undergoing a change: his approach became broader and more experimental, and he frequently, but not always successfully, tried to introduce a sense of movement into his portraits. When faced in 1782 with the commission to paint the Baccelli, a dancer and the essence of graceful movement, the result was a uniquely harmonious combination of painter, sitter and technique. It would not have been very like Gainsborough to search for stylistic precedents on which he could base his composition, as Sir Joshua Reynolds would have inevitably done; it is evident that he painted the Baccelli as she was, dressed for her part in her great success of the 1781–2 season *Les Amans Surpris* (complete with stage make-up), executing a specific dance movement. One only has to compare her pose with those portrayed by Levitsky in the 1770s in his splendid series of full-lengths of the favourite ladies of Catherine the Great dancing in amateur productions of the very same French ballets that Baccelli performed profession-ally, to see that the movements (the Baccelli's included) practic-ally run into each other, like illustrations of how to dance the minuet.

The great difference that would come out in the comparison would, of course, be Gainsborough's uniquely personal style of handling paint. Recent cleaning of the painting has fully re-vealed the sparkle of the rapid and light brush strokes, in places as delicate as a water colour, which give substance to the tradition that Gainsborough worked very fast, with paints so thin that he had to take care to keep his palette level to stop them from running off. The composition is built up – instinctively, one feels – to move round the figure in a slow spiral, from the pointed toe in the pool of light in front, following the folds of the skirt behind the back of the figure and cascading down from the out-stretched arm in the folds of the decorative apron. Gainsborough usually worked out his compositions directly on the canvas and the existence of an oil sketch for the Baccelli shows that he regarded the painting as something of a challenge. Even so we can see that he made certain alterations on the large canvas to the arm which Baccelli holds behind her back, as well as to the outstretched hand. The banked-up clouds and the flying ribbons reinforce the main movement of the figure. In the beginning the entire figure probably stood out sharply against the sky (as in the sketch in the Beit collection) but this gave too much emphasis to the outstretched arm, taking away attention from the magni-ficent head. Gainsborough shifted the emphasis by raising up the dark tree background to engulf the hand. That the trees were originally meant to be only half their height is shown not only by the Beit sketch, but also by the scale of their trunks in relation to their height. The essence of the portrait is summed up to perfection by the contemporary newspaper critic who wrote that it 'is as the Original, light airy and elegant'.

One could add that the poetic quality of Gainsborough's brush would make it a great portrait of a dancer even if we did not know who the sitter was, though the artist makes no attempt to give anything more than a likeness.

Reynolds' portrait, on the other hand, painted for the Duke the following year, in 1783, subjects the sitter to an elaborate programme of Venetian colouring and allusions to Dionysiac revels (wine leaves) and the stage (mask) that make the likeness almost irrelevant. Thus in more prudish times his painting could remain safely in the public eye as 'A Bacchante', while the Gainsborough for all its elegance, being uniquely Baccelli herself, had at times to share the banishment of Locatelli's too-explicit statue. It is as if the Duke considered that Reynolds (and later one of the heirs of his style, Hoppner) was the appropriate painter of the public image of the ducal family and their connections, presenting them in the way in which they wanted to be seen by posterity in the context of their status, while Gainsborough could be entrusted only with a more intimate product that merely caught the likeness and equipped the sitter with no more than his or her own personality. If he felt this, he made the right distinction between the rhetoric and poetry of painting, but he was probably wrong as to which he expected to speak louder down the ages.

Gainsborough's Baccelli remained at Knole until 1890, when it was sold privately to S. Cunliffe-Lister, later Lord Masham. With the sale of the paintings from the Swinton estates in 1975, the portrait came, through the good offices of Messrs Christie's, to the Tate Gallery.

I hope you will not return by that vile country [France]. I begin to hate the name of the country as I lose having any opinion of any of the inhabitants. They are almost *all intriguing, low, artful and treacherous people. They show it now in London, even the aristocrats for malgré qu'ils sont ici et qu'ils passent leur temps agréablement et tranquillement, il n'y a point de mal qu'ils ne nous emportent. They call She–n [Sheridan] le roi des democrates. and are delighted with his sentiments . . . We must take care or else democracy will gain ground . . .*

The Duke of Dorset to Georgiana, Duchess of Devonshire, 29 March 1792. *The Correspondence of Georgiana, Duchess of Devonshire,* ed. The Earl of Bessborough, 1955, p.190

March 9, 1797
Mr. Sackville, the Duke of Dorset's son by Madame Bacelli (the celebrated dancer), while an ensign in the Army married the daugr. of a Pastry Cook at St. Edmundsbury. He afterwards was sent to Gibraltar and returning to England, the Duke obliged him to go to the West Indies with a view to promoting him. There soon after His arrival he caught the yellow fever and died.

Farington Diary, ed. J.Greig, I, p.199.

Postscript

Madame Baccelli, who for so many years distinguished herself as one of the most fascinating dancers that ever appeared on the Opera stage, died at her lodgings in Sackville Street on Thursday morning, after a most lingering and painful illness, which she bore with the most exemplary resignation, and with that sweetness of temper which rendered her so attracting in the days of her youth and beauty.

Morning Chronicle, 9 May 1801.

Obituaries: 7 May 1801:
In Sackville-street, Piccadilly, Madame Baccelli, many years principal dancer at the Opera-house, and generally respected for her benevolence. She lived several years with the late Duke of Dorset who had by her a son, who died, about two years since, in the royal navy.

Gentleman's Magazine, June 1801

Baccelli was not very fortunate in her descendants. Her son by the Duke of Dorset, John Frederick Sackville, born probably in 1779, received all the benefits of a gentleman's upbringing in a noble household and promised to turn out well. He is said to have greatly resembled his handsome father, and a fiercely anti-French patriotic poem, signed 'J. F. Sackville hoc composuit Sept. 25th 1792' (*A History of the Woodgate Family*, 1911, p. 165), shows that he was brought up to share his views in many things. He remained at Knole after his mother's departure in 1789, attended school at Sevenoaks and then embarked on an army career as a lieutenant and later captain in the 69th (South Lincolnshire) Regiment of Foot. The regiment was at Port au Prince, Santo Domingo, between 1796 and 1798 and here, on 24 December 1796, the young captain succumbed to 'a deadly feaver', along with some twenty-five other officers and 800 men.

Before his departure for the West Indies, John Frederick blotted his copy-book somewhat by a rash liaison with an Amy Skoulding (later probably Mrs Delatre) who had a son by him, Sackville Sackville, on 24 February 1796. Quite possibly Farington was right in repeating current gossip that she was the daughter of a pastry-cook in Bury St. Edmunds, and clearly this was not an approved connection. The ducal family had no interest in the boy, and although Baccelli proved a devoted and probably over-indulgent grandmother, she saw to it that the boy's mother should in no way benefit from her will. After her death the child was sent to school in Lowestoft, where he proved impervious to education, his manners became 'quite neglected', he acquired an objectionable provincial accent and showed himself so unreliable and weak-willed that it was thought best to conceal from him the fact that he was one of his grandmother's heirs until such a time when he had learnt to be

more prudent. 'We could, indeed, scarcely expect that it should
be otherwise' wrote Captain Delatre, his foster-father, in 1810,
'as his Grandmother, the most good and worthy woman, could
not be thought nor long to maintain the authority necessary . . .'.
Finally, Sackville went with the Delatres to India, where after a
bad start in the East India Company, he entered the army and
was sent to Ceylon. There, at Badula, on 25 November 1815, he
died of 'a remittant fever' while 'looked after in the Com-
mandant's own quarters with greatest kindness'. He was,
apparently, genuinely regretted by the Delatres, as 'his conduct
since he had visited us had been such as to give us confident
hopes that he would become an amiable and worthy member of
society'.

John Bianchi, Baccelli's nephew, who was largely brought up
with her son and who was also one of her legatees, is described
in a copy of his death certificate as 'Charles Jean Mathieu
Bianchi fils de Jean Baptiste Bianchi et Demoiselle Francoise
Claude Zanerini, sa femme'. It further tells us that he was a
musician, had been born at Paris, and died at Neuilly, France, in
1802, at the age of 27. It is quite likely that his father is identical
with Giovanni Bianchi, musical director of the King's Theatre,
Haymarket, from *c.*1780 onwards.

1a J. Thornthwaite after
James Roberts
*Signora Baccelli in the Ballet
(call'd) Les Amans Surpris*

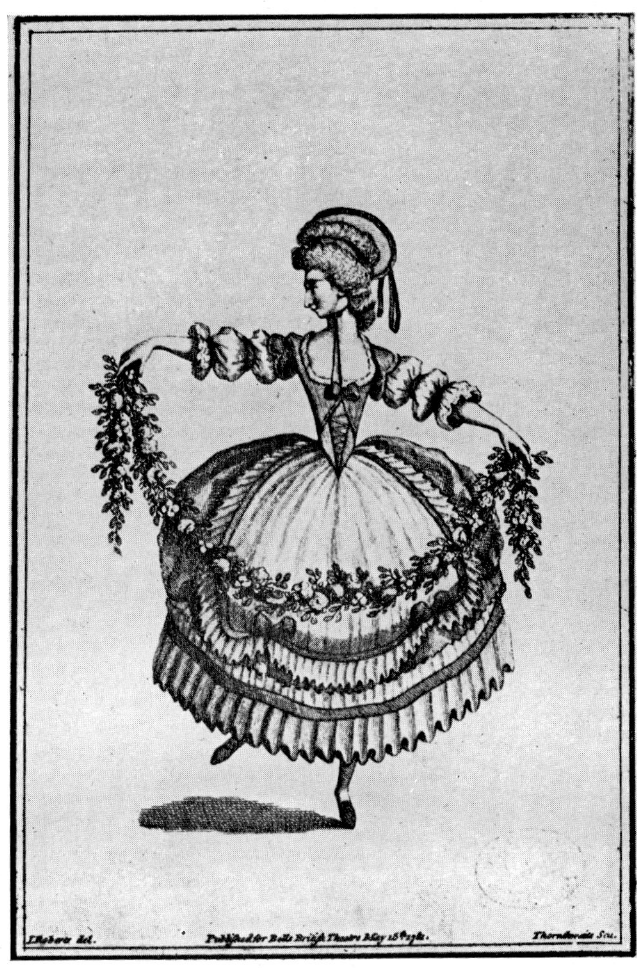

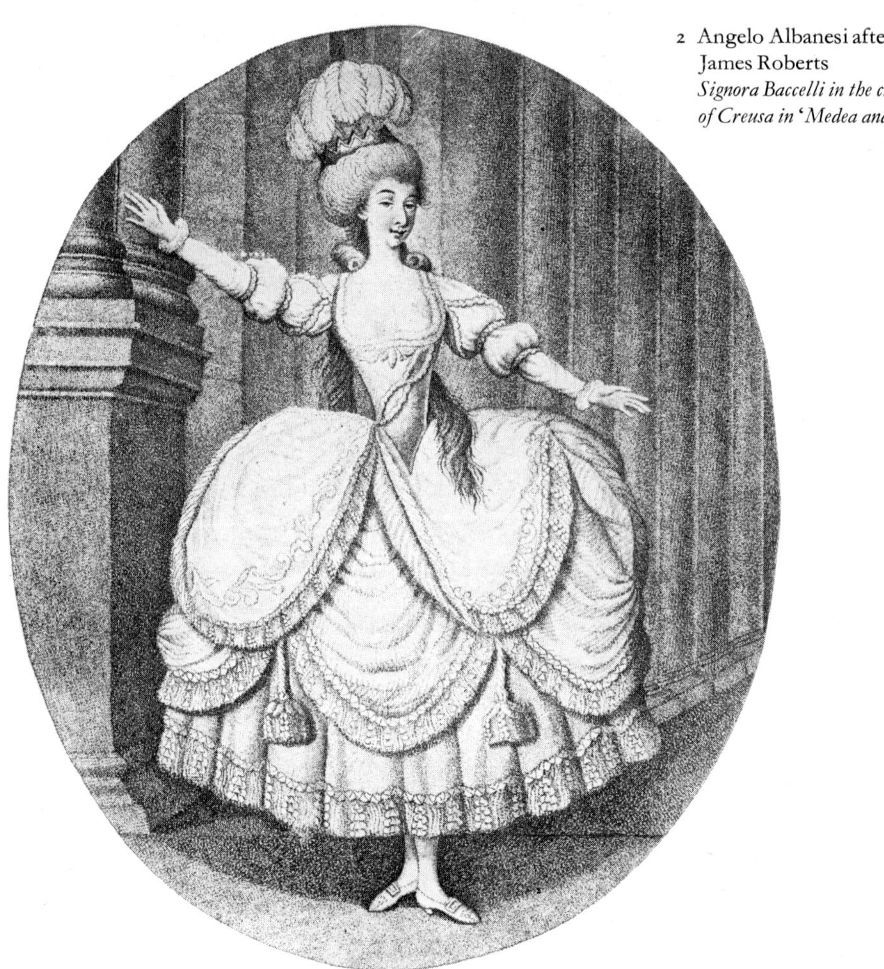

2 Angelo Albanesi after
James Roberts
*Signora Baccelli in the character
of Creusa in 'Medea and Jason'*

9 Thomas
Gainsborough
*John Frederick
Sackville, 3rd
Duke of Dorset*

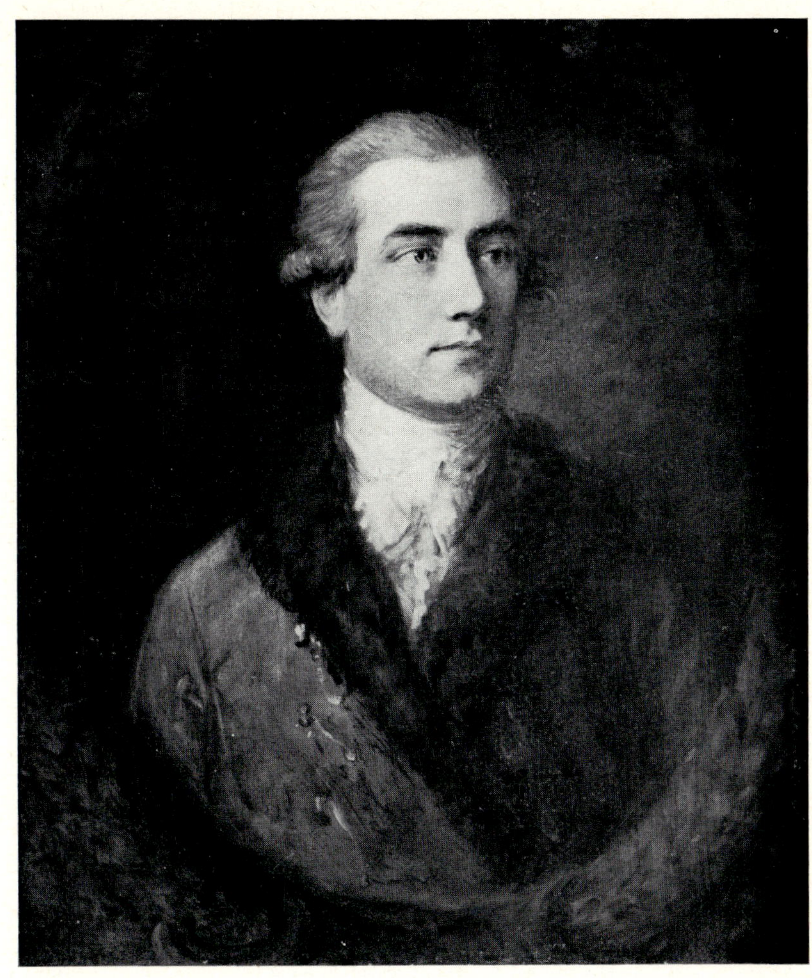

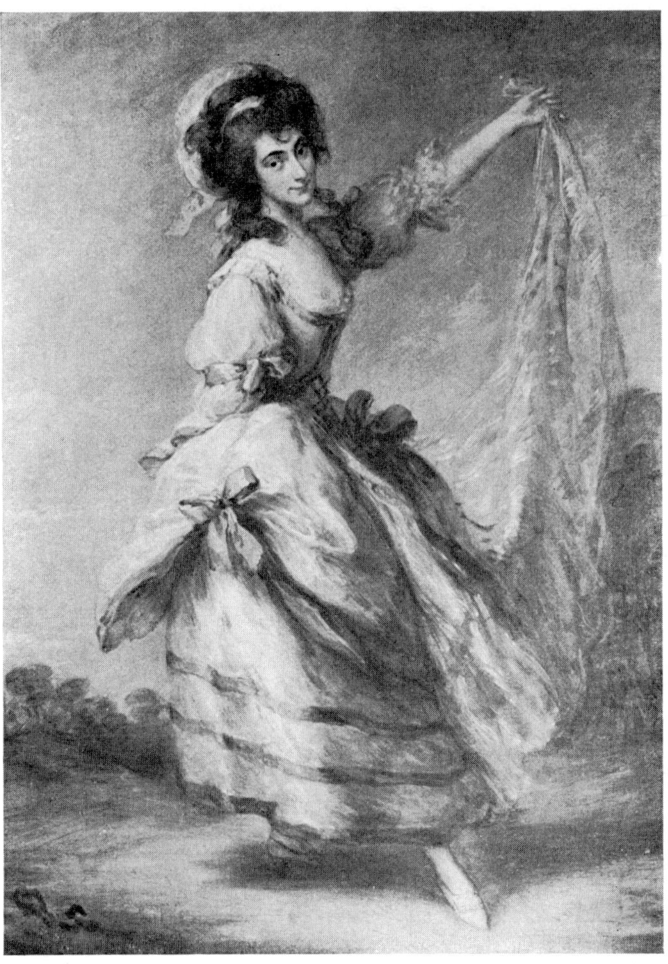

11 Thomas Gainsborough
Giovanna Baccelli

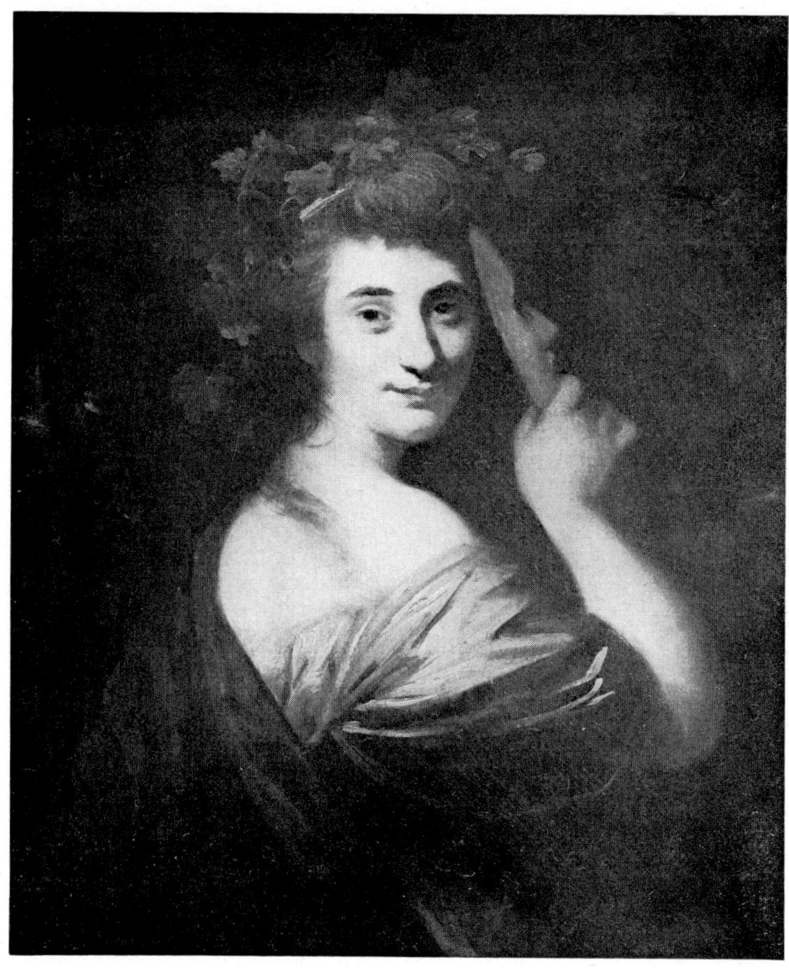

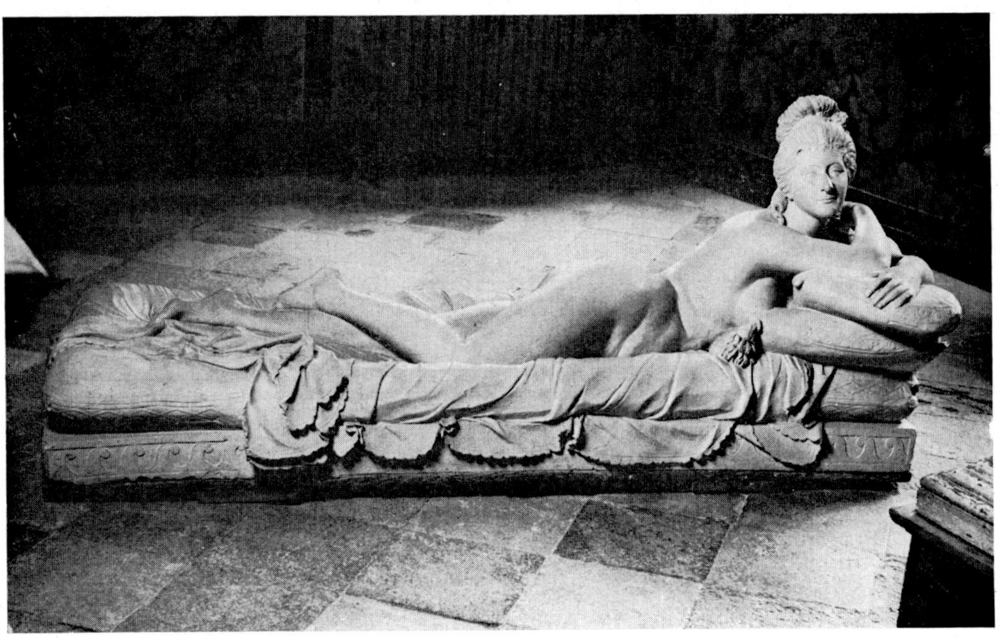

14 Ozias Humphry
Signora Baccelli

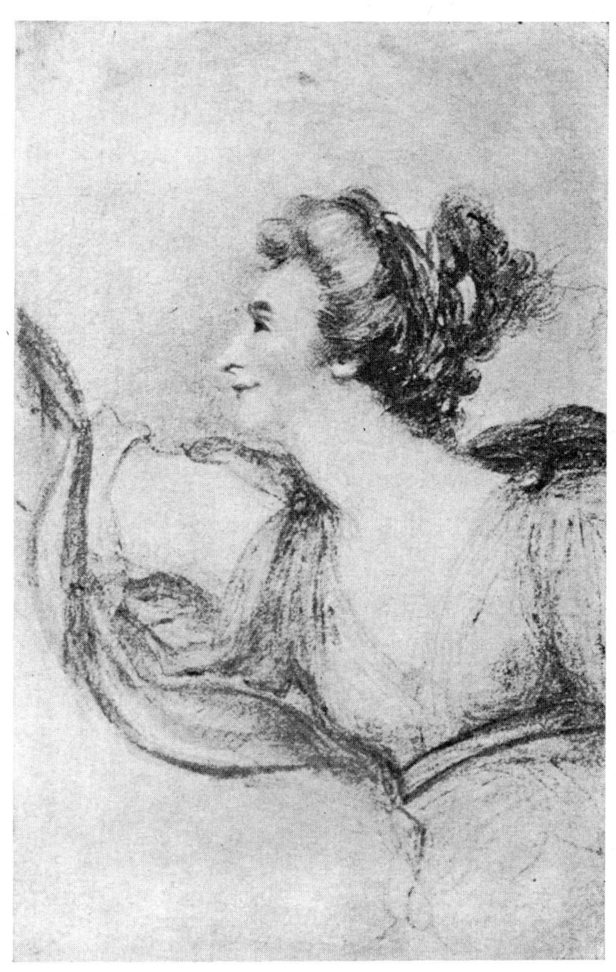

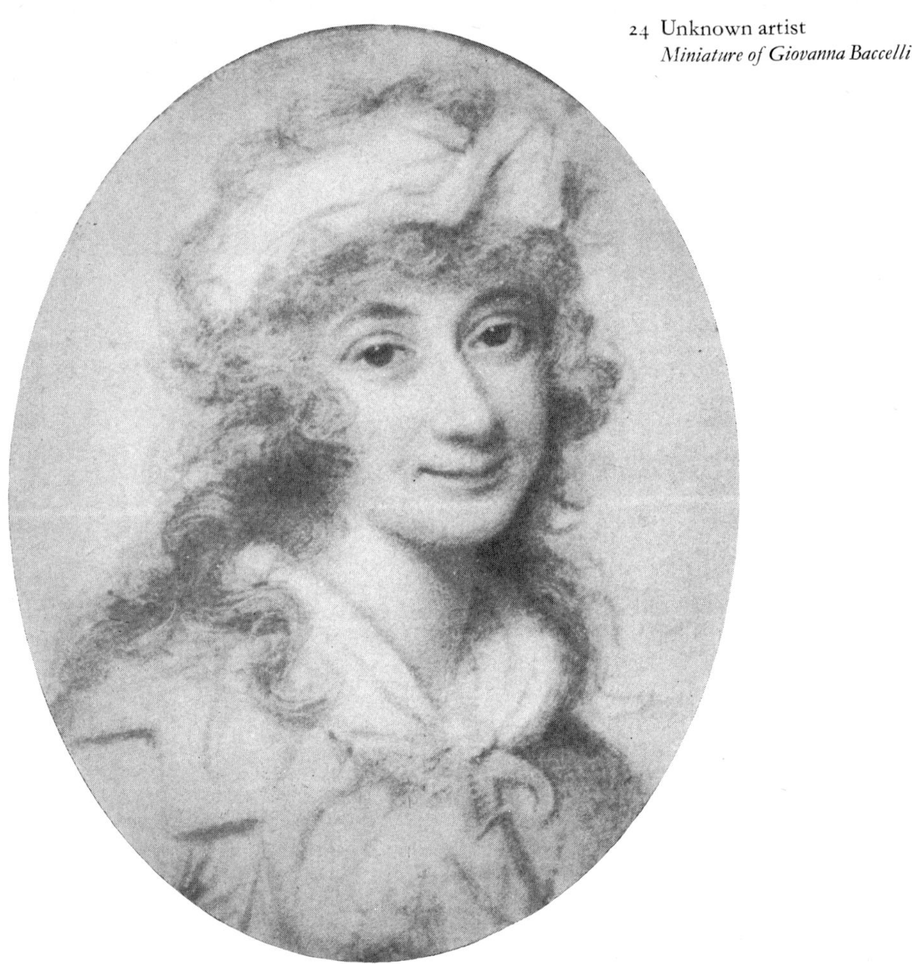

24 Unknown artist
Miniature of Giovanna Baccelli

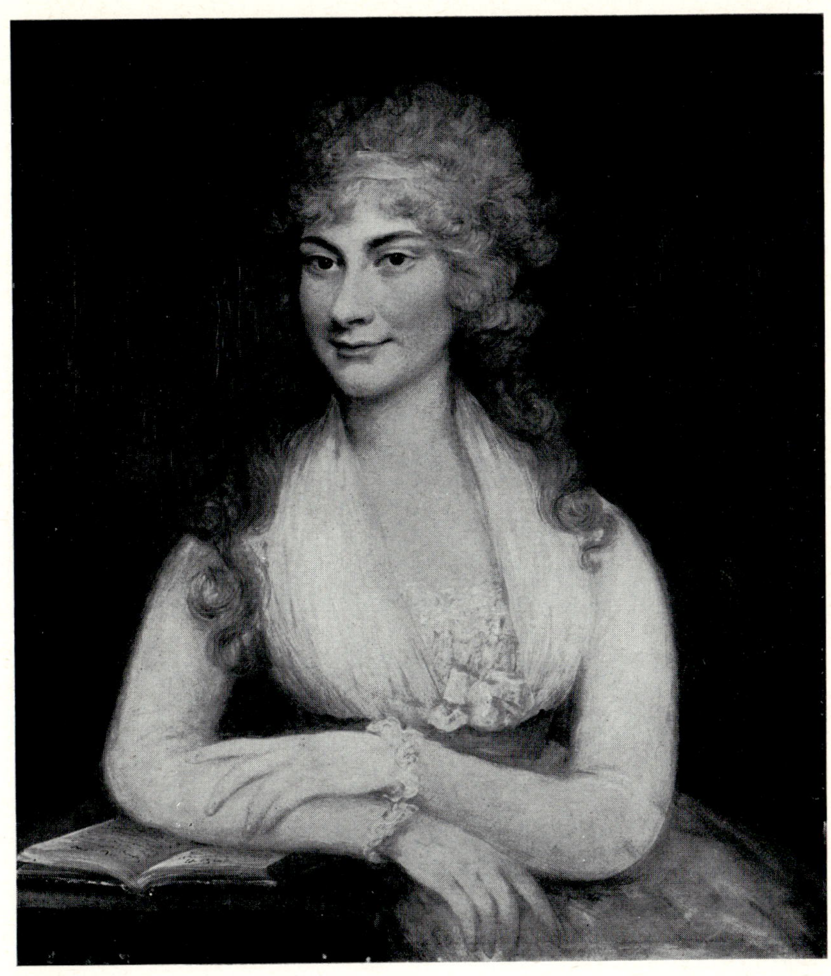

26 Gainsborough
Dupont
Giovanna Zanerini,
'*La Baccelli*'

Catalogue

Sizes are given in inches and centimetres, height
before width

1 J. THORNTHWAITE (fl.1771–95) after
    JAMES ROBERTS (c.1725–99)

a **Signora Baccelli in the Ballet (call'd) Les
Amans Surpris**
Stipple and line engraving cut to 6×4
(15.5×10.5)
Writing engraving: title and 'I. Roberts del.
Published for Bells British Theatre May 15th
1781. Thornthwaite scu.'

b **Monsr. Vestris Junr. in the Favourite
Ballet (call'd) Les Amans Surpris**
As above, but dated 20 July 1781, and cut
down along right margin
Lit: Ivor Guest, 1957, Baccelli repr.; Brian
Reade, *Ballet Designs and Illustrations 1581–
1940*, HMSO, 1967, p.20, No.64 (for Baccelli)
repr.
Theatre Museum

The costume of Baccelli in this print has so
many points of similarity with that in Gainsborough's great full-length, that it is safe to
assume that Gainsborough portrayed her in her
role as Auguste Vestris' partner in *Les Amans
Surpris*. The ballet was first produced at the
King's Theatre on 16 December 1780, with
choreography by Simonet, then ballet master of
the theatre.

2 ANGELO ALBANESI (fl. c.1750–1800) after
    JAMES ROBERTS (c.1725–99)
**Signora Baccelli in the character of
Creusa in 'Medea and Jason'**
Published by I. Harris, 1782
Engraving, upright oval, stipple bistre print,
cut margins, $7\frac{1}{16} \times 5\frac{3}{8}$ (18×13.7)
Writing engraving: title and 'I. Roberts delt
Albanesi sc.'
Lit: Ivor Guest, 1957, repr.
*The Raymond Mander and Joe Mitchenson
Theatre Collection*

3 FRANCESCO BARTOLOZZI, R.A. (1727–
1815) possibly after NATHANIEL DANCE,
R.A. (later Sir N. Dance-Holland, Bt.) (1734–
1811)
Jason et Médée. Ballet Tragique
Writing engraving: 'Published July 3rd 1781
by John Boydell Engraver in Cheapside
London.'
Etching and aquatint in two shades of
brown, $16\frac{7}{16} \times 18\frac{3}{4}$ (41.8 × 47.6)
Lit: Ivor Guest, 1957, repr.; Brian Reade
Ballet Designs and Illustrations 1581–1940,
HMSO, 1967, No.67, repr.
Department of Prints and Drawings,
Victoria and Albert Museum

This satirical print shows Gaëtan Vestris (1729–
1808) in his production of Noverre's *Médée
et Jason* which was shown at the King's Theatre,
Haymarket, March–June 1781, with Vestris and
Madame Simonet in the title roles, and Baccelli
as Creusa. The ballet was such a success that it
was accorded the ultimate compliment of a
burlesque at the Theatre Royal, Haymarket,
opposite King's. The fact that Vestris claimed
the grand production as his own work was not
lost on the public, and one can be sure that the
dances 'by Novestris' included in the burlesque
sent up the mannerisms of the principal dancers.
It is very likely that the above print was produced
in July as a puff for the burlesque, which was
performed throughout August and September.
The costumes in this ballet–which, in the male
costumes at least, still recall quasi-Roman
'heroic' dress–were designed by Novosielski,
who in 1782 redesigned the whole interior of
the King's Theatre along neo-classic lines.

Creusa was one of Baccelli's 'heavy' roles, and
Ivor Guest's description of it can hardly be
bettered: '. . . her rendering of the tragic role of
Creusa in *Médée et Jason*, in the words of one
critic, "wound up our wonder and distress to
the highest pitch." Creusa was the unfortunate
princess whom Jason was to marry after his
separation from Medea, but who died in burn-
ing torment after Medea had given her a
poisoned garment: in the ballet this instrument
of murder was replaced by a lethal nosegay.
Alongside Gaëtan Vestris himself playing the
part of Jason and Madame Simonet portraying
the revengeful Medea with great passion and
energy, Baccelli, as Creusa, was "all gentleness
and graces", wrote the *Public Advertiser*, "and
in perfect contrast with the haughty, inhuman
Princess of Colchos (Medea). Creusa's dying
scene, when she falls victim to the deadly effects
of the fatal nosegay, might serve as an useful
lesson to our best tragedians".'

attributed to
4 GAINSBOROUGH DUPONT (1754–97)
Marie-Auguste Vestris
Oil on canvas, $12\frac{1}{2} \times 10\frac{1}{2}$ (31.8 × 26.7)
Tate Gallery (1480)
In false oval, with white stock and brown coat.
The identification of the sitter as Vestris junior
is of long standing and quite acceptable. A more
recent identification by Charles Merril Mount
as the painter Gilbert Stuart on grounds of likeness is untenable, as Stuart had grey eyes while
the sitter's are clearly brown. The painting
appears to be related to the portrait of Vestris by
Thomas Gainsborough, sold in Paris, 20 May

1905 (repr. *Burlington Magazine*, VII, 1905, p.256).

The Vestris, father and son, were perhaps the most eminent and certainly the most popular dancers whom Giovanna Baccelli partnered at the King's Theatre, Haymarket. Their first appearance there in 1781 took the public by storm and, as one of the leading female dancers, Baccelli naturally shared their success.

5 WILLIAM CAPON (1757–1827)
Interior of the King's Theatre, Haymarket in 1785
Pencil and watercolour, $7\frac{3}{4} \times 9\frac{1}{4}$ (19.7 × 23.5)
Lit: *Survey of London,* XXIX (Parish of St. James Westminster, Part I, S. of Piccadilly), p.230; repr. in Vol.XXX (Part II), pl.25b
University of Bristol Theatre Collection
(Richard Southern Accession)
The view shows the interior of the theatre after Michael Novosielski's alterations of 1782, with the pit and stage arranged for a masquerade in 1785. A note in Capon's hand states that the picture was painted in 1820, but measured and drawn by him in 1785, when he 'assisted Mr. Novosielski in some parts of the decoration'.

6 THOMAS ROWLANDSON (1756–1827)
The Prospect Before Us No.2 1791
Published by S. W. Fores of Piccadilly, 13 January 1791
Coloured engraving, cut margins, 12 × 18 (30.5 × 45.7)
Theatre Museum
The engraving shows the interior of the King's Theatre at the Pantheon (at this time a serious rival of the King's Theatre, Haymarket) in 1791,

during a performance of the ballet *Amphion and Thalia,* with Didelot and Mlle Theodore (both former colleagues of Baccelli) as the leading dancers. Although Baccelli herself was no longer dancing by this time, the scene conveys well the atmosphere of the performance of a pastoral ballet before a packed audience towards the end of the century.

7 **Score of opera dances performed at the King's Theatre, Haymarket** 1781–3
Lord Sackville
The scores, which have been bound somewhat haphazardly, include:

a. 'The celebrated Dances Performed by the Messrs Vestris & C. at the King's Theatre in the Hay Market 1781. Composed by G. B. Noferi, Book II', with solo passages for 'Sigr Vestris Junr & Sigra Bacchelli' and other dancers.

b. Book III. Dances from *Medea and Jason.*

c. Book I. 'Opera Dances as performed at the King's Theatre for the Harpsichord, Violin & Co. 1783. Composed by Sig. Borghi & others'.

d. 'A Choice Collection of the most Favorite French Songs as Sung at the Comedie Italienne at Paris.'

8 **Plan of the boxes at the King's Theatre, Haymarket** 1798
Pocket volume, bound in green silk, 5 × 3 (12 × 7.6)
Lord Sackville
The engraved title page reflects the neo-classic

Adamesque influences in theatre design and décor that prevailed at the end of the century.

Although Giovanna Baccelli was now living in retirement, some of the names would have been familiar to her. Her relative Signor Bianchi is still the company's 'Composer', there are boxes reserved for the Earl and Countess of Pembroke, Sir John Macpherson, and one shared, with others, by the current Duke of Dorset and Earl Cowper, all families at one time more or less intimately connected with her.

John Frederick Sackville, 3rd Duke of Dorset

---

9 THOMAS GAINSBOROUGH, R.A. (1727–88)
John Frederick Sackville, 3rd Duke of Dorset 1782
Oil on canvas, 30 × 25 (76.2 × 63.5)
Coll: Painted for the sitter in 1782. Thence by descent
Lit: E. K. Waterhouse, *Gainsborough*, 1958, p.203, No.203, repr. pl.251
Lord Sackville

John Frederick Sackville (1745–99) inherited Knole and a considerable fortune from his uncle in 1769. Remarkably handsome and charming, he spent much time in Italy and France and had a succession of famous mistresses – among them Nancy Parsons, Mrs Elizabeth Armistead, the Countess of Derby and, last and longest, Giovanna Baccelli. He was British envoy in France from 1783 until the French Revolution in 1789, and then married the heiress Arabella Diana Cope in 1790. From the late 1780s, a mood of depression and melancholy seems to have become dominant in his character, possibly as the after effects of a stroke in 1785, and he died in 1799, according to Wraxall, 'in a state of intellectual decay or mental alienation'. In his younger days he was a keen cricketer, did much to restore the neglected fabric of Knole and to replant its park, and acquired many works of art for the collection. He also patronised living artists, notably musicians, and painters like Reynolds, Gainsborough, Romney, Humphry, Opie and others. He was, incidentally, one of the pall-bearers at Reynolds' funeral in 1792.

This splendid portrait seems to have been part of a 'bulk order' to Gainsborough and painted at the same time as the full-length of Baccelli. According to current newspaper reports, it was also destined for the R.A. in 1782, but was not, in the event, shown, possibly for reasons of decorum. There are records at Knole of Gainsborough's receipt for the group of pictures in which this is included:

'Recd. of His Grace the Duke of Dorset one hundred Guineas in full for two ¾ Portraits of his Grace, one full length of Madlle Baccelli, two Landskips and one sketch of Begger Boy and Girl £105. June 15 1784/ Tho. Gainsborough'

The payment seems very small for five pictures, but it could be the last part of a larger payment, even if this is not stated explicitly in the receipt. The receipt does suggest, however, that there was an autograph replica of this portrait, and one is tempted to think that this

could be the 'late Duke of Dorsett's picture'
bequeathed by Giovanna Baccelli to the banker
George Stone, who was so intimately concerned
in both the Duke's and Baccelli's financial affairs.
No trace remains, alas, of the landscapes, or the
sketch of a beggar boy and girl.

10 THOMAS GAINSBOROUGH, R.A. (1727–88)
Giovanna Baccelli
Oil on canvas, 89 × 58⅜ (226.1 × 148.3)
Inscribed 'Madam B' in ink on back of
canvas
Coll: Painted for John Frederick Sackville,
3rd Duke of Dorset; remained at Knole,
Sevenoaks, until 1890, when sold privately
to S. Cunliffe-Lister (later Lord Masham);
purchased from the Trustees of the Swinton
Settled Estates, via Christie, Manson &
Woods Ltd, 1975, with a contribution from
the Friends of the Tate Gallery.
Exh: R.A., 1782 (230); *Old Masters*, R.A.,
1872 (56); Berlin, 1908 (57); Cartwright Hall,
Bradford, 1925; Ipswich, 1927 (54, repr.
pl.viii); *British Art*, R.A., 1934 (176);
A Hundred Years of the Royal Academy, R.A.,
1951 (221)
Lit: G. W. Fulcher, *Gainsborough*, 1856, p.185;
Sir W. Armstrong, *Gainsborough*, 1904,
p.258; W. T. Whitley, *Gainsborough*, 1915,
pp.180, 184–5, 188, 244; V. Sackville-West,
Knole and the Sackvilles, 1922, pp.189–92;
C. J. Phillips, *History of the Sackville Family*,
1929, II, pp.190, 192, 200–2, 343, 407, 412,
436; *Commemorative Catalogue of the [R.A.]
Exhibition of British Art 1934*, p.56, No.201;
I. Kyrle Fletcher 'An Unpublished Letter

from Dauberval' in *Theatre Notebook*, IV,
October 1949–July 1950, p.5; I. Guest 'The
Italian Lady at Knole' in *Ballet Annual*,
No.11, 1957, p.78, repr.; E. K. Waterhouse,
Gainsborough, 1958, pp.28, 52, No.29, repr.
pl.235; J. Hayes, *Gainsborough Paintings and
Drawings*, repr. pls.128 (col.) and 132 (detail)
Tate Gallery (T.2000)

11 THOMAS GAINSBOROUGH, R.A. (1727–88)
Giovanna Baccelli
Oil on canvas, 22 × 15½ (56 × 39.4)
Coll: Possibly in Gainsborough's studio
1785, and possibly the picture sold by
J. Johnson at Christie's 15 April 1842 (151)
as 'Madame Bucella' and bought by Bulteel.
Sold at Forster's c.1847 as 'Miss Farren';
Henry Harrison sale, Foster's 13 May 1896
(137) as 'Maria Darlington', bt. Wertheimer;
Alfred Beit 1896
Exh: Agnew's Galleries in London 1896,
Paris 1900, and Berlin 1908; *English
Conversation Pieces*, 25 Park Lane, 1930 (147);
Ipswich 1927 (72)
Sir Alfred Beit Bt.
Small sketch for the big Tate version of 1782.
Note the rough blob in the bottom left corner,
adumbrating the tambourine and roses in the
finished version, the different rendering of the
outstretched hand and the much lower background trees. It is possible that Gainsborough
retained this sketch in his studio, as he did the
oil sketch (now in the Royal Collection) for his
portrait of 'Perdita' Robinson (Wallace Collection), also painted in 1782. W. T. Whitley quotes
the *Morning Herald*, 29 June 1785: 'Madame St.

Alban is at this time sitting to Mr. Gainsborough and surveys, with triumphant air, the portrait of the toe-poised Baccelli, which is placed in the Gallery of that distinguished painter'. Whitley clearly thinks the big version of 1782 is referred to, but that is unlikely to have been still in the painter's studio in 1785.

Madame St. Alban is generally thought to be Grace Dalrymple, later Mrs Elliott, mistress of the Earl of Cholmondeley and the Prince of Wales. Baccelli had a portrait of 'Madame St. Albin' among her paintings, and, as 'Dally the Tall' (as she was called by the newspapers) spent much time in France, it is quite possible that the two ladies were friends.

12 SIR JOSHUA REYNOLDS, P.R.A. (1723–92)
Giovanna Baccelli as a Bacchante
Oil on canvas, $29\frac{3}{8} \times 24\frac{1}{8}$ (75.5 × 61.4)
Coll: Painted for the 3rd Duke of Dorset, thence by descent
Engr: J. R. Smith (oval) 1783; G. Sanders 1867
Exh: R.A. 1783 (206); Guelph exhibition, New Gallery, 1891 (148)
Lit: A. Graves and V. Cronin, *Reynolds*, 1899, I, p.41; C. J. Phillips 1929, II, repr. f.p.200; E. K. Waterhouse, *Reynolds*, 1941, p.74
Lord Sackville

Graves and Cronin quote an undated review of the 1783 Royal Academy exhibition in the *Morning Chronicle* which considered the painting had 'much truth of likeness, but not of the most captivating kind'. One is inclined to agree. They also record sittings in 1782–3, and a payment of £52. 10s by the Duke in February 1783.

A copy of this painting (30 × 25 in) was sold at Christie's, 6 June 1896 (93).

13 JOHN BAPTIST LOCATELLI (1735–1805)
Giovanna Baccelli reclining on a Couch
Plaster, life size
Lit: R. Gunnis, *Dictionary of British Sculptors*, 1953, p.240; A. Graves, *Royal Academy . . . Contributors*, 1906, V, p.78
The National Trust (Knole, Sevenoaks)

Locatelli, who worked in England *c.*1775–96, exhibited a 'Bust of Mademoiselle Baccelli' at the Royal Academy in 1781 (516), which is probably the same as the 'Bust of Bacelli' by Locatelli' still recorded by George Scharf on a visit to Knole on 24 September 1874 (Scharf sketch book No.92, p.50, National Portrait Gallery). This is no longer at Knole and its present whereabouts is unknown.

Gunnis seems to think that this figure postdates the bust by one or two years, and suggests that the 'female figure lying on a couch as large as life, modelled by Locatelli from nature', which Hughson saw in the showrooms of Mrs Coade's Artificial Stone Manufactory at Lambeth (*London*, IV, p.545) could have been a terracotta cast either for the signed marble Venus now at Stratfield Saye, or for the Knole statue. The treatment of both is very similar and wholly characteristic of Locatelli's style, which was nicely summed up by the *Morning Herald*'s reviewer of the R.A. exhibition of 1782 (22 May) when he tersely described No.482 (which must have been a very similar work entitled 'Venus'), as 'very fleshy, and seems to sink into the mattrass and pillows'.

Not surprisingly, soon after the Duke's death, the statue was inventoried merely as 'A Naked Venus, whole length, plaister', and spent the nineteenth century and the beginning of the twentieth tucked away in the servants' attic.

14 OZIAS HUMPHRY R.A. (1743–1810)
Signora Baccelli
Photograph of a drawing in sanguine,
$5 \times 3\frac{1}{8}$ (12.2 × 8)
Formerly in the C. Hampden Turner collection, present whereabouts unknown
Lit: G. C. Williamson, 1918, pp. 93, 101–2, repr. (in col.) f.p. 162; L. A. Hall, *Catalogue of Dramatic Portraits in the Theatre Collection of the Harvard College Library*, 1930, p. 44, repr.

In 1780 Humphry exhibited at the Royal Academy (No. 335) 'A portrait of a lady in the character of Iris', identified in Walpole's notes as 'Signora Baccelli'. The painting is not starred in the catalogue as being for sale, and it appears to have been painted for the Duke of Dorset, though its subsequent history is not known. Williamson quotes a letter from the artist to his brother at Sevenoaks, apparently dated 17 March 1780, to the effect that the painting of Baccelli was 'not well placed and therefore remarkably ill seen . . . its effect of course not half so agreeable as in my room'. Humphry, who had been extensively patronised by the Duke since the 1760s, goes on to say, with reference to the picture, that the Duke, when he called upon him, had mentioned that 'Prince Frederick Bishop of Osnaburgh' had thought it 'a very fine likeness' and 'a good picture'. Iris was the part danced by Baccelli in the 1779 season at King's Theatre in the ballet *La Fête du Ciel*. It is possible that the above drawing is related to the lost painting. Williamson dates the drawing to 1789, which is unlikely, as it was engraved as an oval by T. Trotter and published by William Holland in 1785. He also says the drawing is 'for the picture now at Knole', but no record of such a picture is to be found.

15 JOHN JONES (1745?–97) after THOMAS GAINSBOROUGH (1727–88)
Signora Baccelli
Published 5 February 1784 by J. Jones of 63 Great Portland Street, Marylebone; same plate reissued in 1814
Mezzotint, $20\frac{7}{8} \times 13\frac{7}{8}$ (50.8 × 35.3)
Lit: C. J. Phillips 1929, repr. f.p. 204
Lord Sackville

The engraver has added the sitter's name on the tambourine in the bottom left hand corner, and a rose to her corsage.

This was evidently one of Baccelli's favourite prints of herself and the Kent Record Office (U269 A 243/20) preserves a bill made out to Baccelli from P. Colnaghi of Torre & Co., Printsellers, for coloured copies of it (cf. No. 20).

16 JOSEPH NASH (1808–78) attributed to
Giovanna Baccelli Posing in the Ballroom at Knole
Pencil and pen on prepared paper (?) laid down on canvas, $35\frac{1}{2} \times 45\frac{1}{2}$ (90 × 115.5)
Lit: C. J. Phillips 1929, 11, repr. f.p. 202
Lord Sackville

The drawing looks like the beginnings of a conversation piece meant to give a romantic impression of how Gainsborough's full-length came to be painted. The two most finished figures, Baccelli and the Chinese boy Wang-Y-Tong, are copied and adapted from the famous Gainsborough and Reynolds paintings at Knole, and the rest of the cosy clutter, very lightly sketched in, clearly tries to reconstruct a supposed colourful chapter in the history of the house.

In fact, Baccelli is much more likely to have sat to Gainsborough in his London studio, nor is the artist likely to have worked on a canvas so strangely draped. The whole approach reminds one of the genre scenes of Joseph Nash, whose work consists mainly of architectural drawings, illustrations to Shakespeare, Scott and Cervantes, and genre in the style of Cattermole. His greatest success was the series of lithographs for the *Mansions of England in Olden Time*, published 1839–49, where he peopled the architectural settings with genre groups often adapted from figures found in the mansions' paintings. These –including the set devoted to Knole–are usually confined to the Tudor period, but he is known to have done eighteenth-century and Victorian settings. In the 1830s he exhibited a number of 'olden time' genre pieces in oils at the Royal Academy, and this sketch could be an abandoned attempt at such a picture.

A cursory search through the massive 1828 inventory at Knole failed to reveal any traces of the drawing, which tends to confirm the supposition that it entered the collection after that date.

17 ALMOND (fl.1783)
Four Portraits of Madame Baccelli's Servants 1783

a Daniel Taylor and Elinor Low
Oil on canvas, $13\frac{3}{4} \times 17\frac{1}{4}$ (35 × 44)
Inscribed on the back with names and 'Servants of Mad^m Baccelli.' and dated 1779 and 1783 respectively

b Andrew Coronin
Oil on canvas, 14×10 (36 × 25.5)
Inscribed on the back with name and 'Vallet to Mad^m Baccelli 1775'

c Mrs Edwards
Oil on canvas, oval $11\frac{1}{2} \times 9\frac{1}{2}$ (29 × 24)
Inscribed on the back with name and 'Attend^t on Mad^m Baccelli'

d Philip Louvaux
Oil on canvas, oval, $11\frac{1}{2} \times 9\frac{1}{2}$ (29 × 24)
Inscribed on back with name and 'Servant to Mad^m Baccelli 1783'

Lit: C. J. Phillips 1929, II, p.444
Lord Sackville

These are part of a set of over twenty portraits of servants at Knole, and more are said to be with other branches of the Sackville family. On the back of one of them is the inscription: 'These portraits were painted at Knole in 1783 by a Mr. Almond, an itinerant painter–I have to each name subjoined the county, the office, and the year he or she came into his Grace's service. J.Bridgman 1793'. The writer was the steward at Knole, and author of the Knole guidebook of 1817. Older inventories at Knole include also a portrait of Ann Davis 'Norce of Master Sackville, Middlesex, 1780', but this has disappeared. Ann Davis is probably the Hannah Davies who was still in Baccelli's employ at her death in 1801.

Andrea Coronin and Mrs Mary Edwards were also still with their mistress in 1801. Under the terms of her will, Coronin received a year's wages and an annuity of £18, which he was paid until his death in 1806. Mrs Edwards was to become more than a servant to Baccelli, who in her will left 'to my friend Mrs Mary Edwards who now lives with me all my Cloaths', an annuity of £20 and 'my Metal Watch & Chain – & my Birds Cage to take care of the Birds that are in it & then sell it'.

18 Book of household accounts at Knole

1779–93
Kent Record Office, Maidstone, lent by kind permission of Lord Sackville
(Cat. U269/A118)

The account book deals with petty household disbursements connected with Madame Baccelli's residence at Knole, that of her son John Frederick Sackville (often referred to in the account-keeper's country-accented and uncertain spelling as 'Marster Sackvell') and of occasional visitors, such as Giovanna's nephew John Bianchi, who stayed from time to time for as long as three weeks. Very frequent postal charges for letters to and from Baccelli show that she was an enthusiastic correspondent, and regular items like 'Comb for the Dogs–6p.' '3 weeks meat for the cats–o. 1. o.' and 'Banten hen for Madam Bacceli–o. 1. 6' show that her fondness for animals was not confined to the inhabitants of her bird-cage in Sackville Street.

There is a vast consumption of lemons (about six or ten a week) which probably served for cosmetic purposes as well as a source of vitamins, and the menu seems to rely chiefly on pigeons, ducks, chicken, oysters, oranges, lobsters, eels and large quantities of fish.

Charges relating to her son speak for a well-cared-for and well-balanced childhood that can be traced over the years from payments for his wet-nurse, through large and regular laundry-bills, purchases of a drum, gingerbread, another drum (the first one lasted four months), 'pair of Spatterdashes', regular haircuts, pair of buckets, to 'Mending Marster Sackvill watch–o. 3.6' and frequent purchases of gloves, until, in February 1787, he graduates to a regular payment of one shilling a month as pocket-money. This was also paid to his cousin John Bianchi, who, on his not infrequent visits, seems to have consumed a lot of combs and gloves. More appropriately, one of the most expensive items in 1788, 'Butts and Stumps–o. 8. 6'–remind one that the boy's noble father was a keen cricketer.

After Baccelli's departure from Knole in December 1789, her name no longer occurs in the accounts, but the frequency of postage paid for 'letters for Mr. Sackvill' rises sharply.

19 Laundry bills for Madame Baccelli, the child, and the nurse Knole, 1783

Kent Record Office, Maidstone, lent by kind permission of Lord Sackville
(Cat. U269/A242/1–3)

**20 Bill from Torre & Co. for prints of
Signora Baccelli**
*Kent Record Office, Maidstone, lent by kind
permission of Lord Sackville*
(Cat. U269/A243/20)
Bill from Torre & Co. (Printsellers) of 132 Pall
Mall, made out by Angelo Coronnini, and
receipted by P. Colnaghi, for '2 Sig^ra Bacelli in
colours by Jones £2. 2. 0' (cf. No.15).

**21 Deed of Settlement granting an annuity
to Giovanna Baccelli** 1785
*Kent Record Office, Maidstone, lent by kind
permission of Lord Sackville*
(Cat. U269/T91/7–9)
The document deals with the grant of an annuity
of £400 by John Frederick, 3rd Duke of Dorset,
to George Stone (his private secretary and
banker) in trust for Signora Giovanna Baccelli,
for her life, charged on property in Withyham
and Hartfield.

In 1789 the charge was transferred to a more
distant part of the Duke's property in Warwick-
shire and Gloucestershire. Possibly it was felt
that, in view of his impending marriage to the
heiress Arabella Diana Cope, such a charge
upon the historic Sackville estates at Withyham
(the Sackville family vaults are in Withyham
church) would be inappropriate.

**22 Photostats of two letters from Giovanna
Baccelli to George Nassau, 3rd Earl
Cowper** (1738–89)
a **from Venice, 29 May 1789**
b **from Knole, 22 August 1789**

*Hertfordshire Record Office, lent by kind
permission of Lady Ravensdale*
The first letter (22a), largely in French, enlists
the Earl's support for a benefit performance in
Florence. She is, apparently, on her way to
Padua, travelling with her mother, Lord Pembroke, and a pet bitch expected to whelp within
the fortnight.

In the second (22b), written largely in Italian
and French, she announces her safe arrival after
a thirty-seven day journey, having returned via
France, where she found 'tutti in arme' and
quite mad. She was therefore unable to fulfil
Lady Cowper's request regarding the latest
Parisian style in bonnets, but would charge the
Duke of Dorset with it as soon as she would see
him. For herself, she would say that any really
crazy concoction would answer the current style
of the nation. . . . She also writes that there can
be no question of dancing in London, as the
Opera House has burnt down and Sir John
Gallini (the manager) is ready to hang himself in
despair.

Madame Baccelli must have been travelling
through France in the chaotic conditions of the
Grande Peur that gripped the country in the
weeks following the fall of the Bastille on 14
July.

23 NATHANIEL DANCE, R.A. (later Sir N. Dance-Holland, Bt.) (1734–1811)
Henry Herbert, 10th Earl of Pembroke (1734–94)
Photograph, by kind permission of the National Portrait Gallery, of painting on canvas, 56 × 46 (142.3 × 116.8)
Coll: Christie's, 18 February 1949 (146). Present whereabouts unknown
Lit: The letters below are quoted from *The Pembroke Papers*, ed. Lord Herbert, 1950, pp.352, 369, 377

Henry, 10th Earl of Pembroke was the other important affair in Giovanna Baccelli's life apart from the Duke of Dorset. The Earl spent much of his life abroad, particularly in Paris and Italy, and his chief interests seem to have been horses and women. On the former he wrote a much respected treatise, *Method of Breaking Horses*, in 1762, which formed the basis of standard methods eventually adopted by the British cavalry. As regards the second, he went through a number of tempestuous and colourful liaisons both at home and abroad, which were borne with patience by his estranged wife and caused great mortification to his son George. Although Baccelli remained on the best of terms with the Duke of Dorset (she did not leave Knole until 1789) her affair with the Earl of Pembroke seems to have taken a serious turn in Paris in 1787. Lord George must have written a complaining letter about this to the family chaplin, Dr Thomas Eyre, who, on 5 July 1787, replied that he was 'really shocked of what you tell me

of an immediate attachment to a new Object wch must disgrace him [the 10th Earl] in the eyes of all Mankind' and expressed the pious hope that his Lordship would be soon 'recovered from his present wise freake with Baccelli.' That hope proved false, and on 18 February 1788 Lord George found cause to write a rather stuffy letter to his disreputable parent:

Dear Lord P.
I cannot help writing to inform you that on going over the House this morning I perceived the portraits [of la Baccelli] in your room which I mentioned to you as being there, on a late very disagreeable transaction. After what passed between you & me on that business, I cannot doubt of your intention to have them taken entirely out of sight, & if you gave orders to anybody to take them away, that person has probably forgot, for which a severe reprimand ought to be given. . . . I therefore have myself removed them, for fear Lady P in particular should visit Wilton, previous to your being here.

The amiable but blustery reply, dated two days later, tells us much about the Earl's character:

Dear George,
I have this moment rec'd yours at Ld Bolingbroke's. . . . To tell you the truth, I never thought more of the prints you mention nor did I give orders to anybody about them. When you took any down, I hope you sealed them up, & left them in some one's care to deliver to me; if not, I beg the favour of you to write to Coward immediately & to give him orders accordingly. To tell you the truth too, I can not look on certain things but as meer

trifling objects, prints etc., of professional people in particular, be they who they may; & as poor Bernard used to say of his lumber room where he sat, I must really have some place, & none surely so fit as my own room, into which nobody need go unless they choose it, where none have any thing to meddle but myself; & one little apartment is not surely an unreasonable refuge to insist upon. And now I am on the topick . . . I cannot forget that on a late bustle, in which I ought to have been the first informed of what was going on, I was the last . . . mais n'importe . . . only I beg order those things, whatever they are, to be sealed up, & *delivered into my own hands*, when I return . . .

 Allways most affecy; your's my
  dear George, P:
Mon ami Mr. d'Albanie kicked the bucket the 31st of last month.

In summer 1789 he was with the Baccelli in Italy, and in 1790 he signed a testamentary bond for £10,000 in her favour. After the Earl's death in 1794, George managed to reduce this by a few thousand, but only by contracting to pay her a small annuity for life (cf. No.25).

When Baccelli died, she left her 'Picture of the Late Lord Pembroke and all the Prints from Pictures in Wilton House' to Col. Le Marchant, later General, a highly respected military colleague of Pembroke's, founder of the Royal Military College, now at Sandhurst.

It may be worth noting that Le Marchant's wife was a Carey, which may explain why Baccelli left her 'Picture of Madame St. Albin' to a Captain Carey, and even the background of the Mr James Carey with whom she spent her last years and who was her chief legatee.

24 Tortoiseshell box mounted with miniatures of Giovanna Baccelli and the 10th Earl of Pembroke
Diameter of box 3¼ (8.3); miniature of Lord Pembroke, oval, 2½ × 2 (6.4 × 5); miniature of Baccelli, oval, 2¼ × 1¾ (5.7 × 4.5)
Mrs Audrey Peake

The box is still in the possession of the descendants of John Turner (d. 1796), Town Clerk of Salisbury and Clerk of the Peace of the County of Wiltshire, who adopted and brought up five illegitimate children, of whom at least three are traditionally thought to have been the offspring of the various liaisons of the 10th Earl of Pembroke. No trace can be found of there having been any children by Baccelli and the Earl, although a death in early infancy could have escaped the records.

The inscription round the Earl's portrait on the lid (after Sir Joshua Reynolds' portrait of 1767–8, still at Wilton) reads: 'TENERO · PADRE · FEDELE · AMICO · APPASSIONATO · AMANTE * HENRY EARL OF PEMBROKE *' which translates as 'tender father, faithful friend, passionate lover'. The portrait of Baccelli on the inside of the lid is by an unknown hand and appears to show her a few years older than in Gainsborough's full-length.

25 Bond signed by 11th Earl of Pembroke undertaking to pay £6,000 to Giovanna Baccelli 1795
Barclays Bank Limited

The bond, dated 15 August 1795, obliges George Herbert, 11th Earl of Pembroke to pay Giovanna Baccelli, 'now of Kensington', a capital sum of £6,000, and £200 per annum for life, on condition that she gives up a previous obligation entered into by his father, the 10th Earl, in 1790, in which he undertook to pay Baccelli, then of Minsteed, Southampton, £10,000. She is, moreover, to keep the £1,000 already paid her by George, and in the case of default on the annual payments, the old bond for £10,000 should become payable.

It seems that Henry, 10th Earl of Pembroke had been particularly generous to Baccelli, especially as it transpires from George Stone's letter of 6 February 1816 (No.29d) that he had already bought French stocks for her in Paris. In view of the political state of France, the income from these would not have been accessible at the time. One can feel some sympathy with George's exasperation and worry at the mixed blessings of his inheritance. These come out clearly in a letter, probably to his banker, dated 5 March 1794, a few months after his father's death:

> Now, I trust, all is out . . . As the Baccelli's Paper turns out to be Testamentary, I am just philosopher enough to thank my stars it is no worse. . . . [I] am not a little anxious to know whereabout I shall stand between affluence & beggary. A beggarly Peer is a bitter bad thing . . .

(Quoted from *The Pembroke Papers*, ed. Lord Herbert, 1950, p.499).

---

26 GAINSBOROUGH DUPONT (1754–97)
Giovanna Zanerini, 'La Baccelli' *c.*1795
Oil on canvas, 29¾ × 24⅞ (75.6 × 63.2)
Coll: Acquired by George IV and recorded in store at Carlton House in 1816 (330: 'A head of Signora Baccelli with a book'), later at Windsor (472)
Exh: *Gainsborough*, Queen's Gallery, 1970 (22)
Lit: J. Hayes, *Connoisseur*, CLXIX (1968) pp.221–7, repr.; O. Millar, *Later Georgian Pictures in the Royal Collection*, 1969, text vol., p.34
Her Majesty The Queen

Half-length, seated at table, leaning on an open book. The lower part seems unfinished.

John Hayes considers that this portrait was painted *c.*1795, when Dupont was working on a series of actors' portraits for Thomas Harris (d. 1820), manager of Covent Garden. It is not, however, part of the Harris series of portraits, all of which portray actors in character. It is possible that it could be the 'Portrait of myself' which Giovanna Baccelli bequeathed in her will to her friend John Humphrey Babb, together with a mourning ring, 'two of the best prints and also the best of the cups of the late Queen of France'.

27 George Stone's memorandum book of events following Giovanna Baccelli's Death 7 May–13 July 1801
Barclays Bank Limited

George Stone, together with his brother

Richard, was an executor of Giovanna Baccelli's will. He was also private secretary, banker and financial adviser to the 3rd Duke of Dorset, and the Stone family owned estates at Chislehurst, Kent, not very far from Knole. Although this hardly shows in his meticulous and formal accounting, George Stone was evidently regarded by his clients as a family friend. Giovanna Baccelli left the Stone brothers 5 gns each for a mourning ring, and bequeathed to George Stone 'the late Duke of Dorsett's picture' (possibly a duplicate of Gainsborough's portrait of the Duke at Knole, the existence of which is suggested in the artist's bill of 1784–cf. No.9), and to his wife Louisa 'my two chandeliers'.

The memorandum book records that on 7 May 1801, Baccelli died 'at 7 o'Clock in the morning after a most painful illness of more than Eight Months duration' and that she was 'interred in the Vault of St. James Church at 9 o'clock in the morning on 13th May, the Funeral being attended by Mr. Carey, Mr. Herrenschwand, Mr. Babb and myself'.

From the wording of the remark on 13 June: 'wrote to the Rev^d Mr. Orgill to mention, for the information of Mrs. Delatre, the bequest to her Son', one could infer that the wife of Captain Delatre (the Delatres were the foster parents of Giovanna Baccelli's grandson, Sackville Sackville, with whom he went to India) was actually Amy Skoulding, named in Baccelli's will as the boy's mother.

28 Passbook of 'Estate of G. Z. Baccelli deceased'
Barclays Bank Limited

It records the administration of Baccelli's estate from her death in 1801 until 1824, when the mysterious Mr James Carey remained the sole legatee. Apart from the legacies and annuities to her servants and her mother, Madame Rosa Baccelli of Treviso, the chief beneficiaries of her not inconsiderable estate (probably in excess of £6,000) were her grandson Sackville Sackville, her nephew John Bianchi, and James Carey Esq.

The book records that although she gave instructions in her will that 'not more than £12 may be expended on my funeral', the cost came in fact to £37. 10, with Mr Carey paying the difference. He also shared her rent and wine bill. Although her pianoforte was sold to Broadwood, Mr Carey bought from her estate the plate, linen, china, books and prints. Her most precious possessions were a pair of pearl bracelets with diamond clasps which were sold, with an antique ring, to 'Gray, Jeweller in Sackville St.' for £360.

She also appears to have had a considerable estate in France, which, because of the Revolution and subsequent hostilities, proved difficult of access.

29 Some banker's documents concerning the Estate of Giovanna Baccelli
Barclays Bank Limited

a. George Stone's list of beneficiaries from her will, dated 5 November 1816.

b. & c. Receipts signed by Andrea Coronin and Hannah Davies, servants to Madame Baccelli.

d. Copy of George Stone's letter, dated 6

February 1816, to Messrs Perregaux, Lafitte & Co. of Paris, 'on the subject of some French stocks belonging to the late Mad. Baccelli'. The stocks, apparently, had been purchased for her by the late Earl of Pembroke.

e. Copy of a letter from George Stone, dated 30 April 1811, setting our some plans for the future career of Sackville Sackville in the East India Company. These came to nothing, and young Sackville went into the army.

General Bibliography

J. Bridgeman, *A Sketch of Knole*, 1817. (George Scharf's annotated copy in the National Portrait Gallery)

Sir Nathaniel Wraxall, *Historical and Posthumous Memoirs*, ed. Wheatley, 1884, IV, pp.30–7 etc.

Walpole Correspondence, ed. Tonybee, 1903

W. T. Whitley, *Gainsborough*, 1915, pp.180, 184–5, 244, 363 (and the Whitley papers, Department of Prints and Drawings, British Museum)

Hugh Stokes, *The Devonshire House Circle*, 1916–7

G. Williams, *Life and Works of Ozias Humphry*, 1918

V. Sackville-West, *Knole and The Sackvilles*, 1922

C. J. Phillips, *History of the Sackville Family*, 1929, II, pp.190, 192, 200–2, 343, 407, 412, 436

The Pembroke Papers, ed. Lord Herbert, 1950

Enciclopedia Dello Spettacolo, Rome, 1954

I. Guest, 'The Italian Lady at Knole', in *The Ballet Annual*, 1957, No. 11

E. K. Waterhouse, *Gainsborough*, 1958

Survey of London, 1960, XXIX (Parish of St. James, Westminster), Part 1, South of Piccadilly, p.230 (for history of the King's Theatre)

J. Hayes, 'Thomas Harris, Gainsborough Dupont and the Theatrical Gallery at Belmont' in *Connoisseur*, 1968, CLXIX, pp.221–7

J. Hayes, *Gainsborough Paintings and Drawings*, 1975